HOW? WHO? WHAT? WHEN? WHERE? WHY?

Questions kids ask

ABOUT
HISTORY

PUBLISHER	Joseph R. DeVarennes	
PUBLICATION DIRECTOR	Kenneth H. Pearson	
ADVISORS	Roger Aubin	
	Robert Furlonger	
EDITORIAL SUPERVISOR	Jocelyn Smyth	
PRODUCTION MANAGER	Ernest Homewood	
PRODUCTION ASSISTANTS	Martine Gingras	Kathy Kishimoto
	Catherine Gordon	Peter Thomlison
CONTRIBUTORS	Alison Dickie	Nancy Prasad
	Bill Ivy	Lois Rock
	Jacqueline Kendel	Merebeth Switzer
	Anne Langdon	Dave Taylor
	Sheila Macdonald	Alison Tharen
	Susan Marshall	Donna Thomson
	Pamela Martin	Pam Young
	Colin McCance	
SENIOR EDITOR	Robin Rivers	
EDITORS	Brian Cross	Ann Martin
	Anne Louise Mahoney	Mayta Tannenbaum
PUBLICATION ADMINISTRATOR	Anna Good	
ART AND DESIGN	Richard Comely	Ronald Migliore
	Robert B. Curry	Penelope Moir
	George Elliott	Marion Stuck
	Marilyn James	Bill Suddick
	Robert Johanssen	Sue Wilkinson

Canadian Cataloguing in Publication Data

Main entry under title:

Questions kids ask about history

(Questions kids ask ; 21)
ISBN 0-7172-2560-7

1. World history—Miscellanea—Juvenile literature.
2. Children's questions and answers.
I. Smyth, Jocelyn.   II. Comely, Richard.   III. Series.

D21.Q48 1988   j909   C89-093170-4

Questions Kids Ask . . . about HISTORY

continued

What started the Klondike Gold Rush?

On August 16, 1896, two prospectors named Skookum Jim and George Washington Carmack found loose gold in the gravel along the Klondike River in the Yukon. They rushed to the nearest town to stake their claims and other prospectors followed their example. Soon claims were staked by prospectors on every creek along the Klondike.

When an American newspaper reported "a ton of gold" in the Klondike, the stampede began. A hundred thousand amateur goldseekers headed for the Yukon from the rest of North America, Europe and Australia!

Yukon gold was "easy" gold. It was found in the river bed as nuggets, flakes and gold dust, or chipped out of veins in rock 10 to 20 metres (30 to 60 feet) deep. But the life of a Klondike prospector was far from easy. Carrying their belongings on their backs, the newcomers faced dense bush, insects, glaciers and mountains. Many people starved or froze to death in winter.

By 1889, the last great gold rush in North America was over. In just three years, millions of dollars had been made and lost in the Klondike Gold Rush.

Why did castles have moats?

You may have heard the expression "a man's home is his castle." Well, in the Middle Ages, the home of a lord or noble really was a castle. It was also a fortress that protected him from attacks by foreign raiders, or even his own neighbors. Around the castle he built a wall and a moat—a wide, deep ditch filled with water—to keep enemies out.

A hinged bridge, or drawbridge, spanned the moat so that the people who belonged in the castle could cross without getting wet. This bridge could be raised or lowered from the castle side of the wall. If he was attacked, the lord raised the drawbridge, and clanged the great gates behind it shut. Then he called his men to hurl stones, arrows and fireballs at the invaders.

DID YOU KNOW. . . .Harlech Castle in Wales was built on a rocky peak and its moat was 9 to 18 metres (30 to 60 feet) wide.

Who were the Crusaders?

The Crusaders were European knights who fought in religious wars called the Crusades, or "wars of the cross."

For centuries, the Holy Land (Palestine) where Jesus had lived was ruled by Arab chiefs who allowed Christians to visit the religious shrines there. In 1070 fierce Muslim Turks (Saracens) seized control of the shrines.

In 1095, the Pope asked Christians of Europe to drive the Saracens out of the Holy Land.

The first Crusaders set out in 1096. Over the next 200 years there were eight Crusades, but the Crusaders failed to recapture the Holy Land.

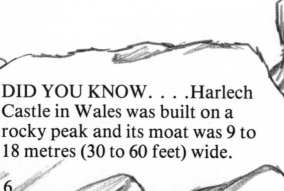

Why did knights wear armor?

Armor was worn to protect knights against their enemies' weapons. Knights of the 13th century wore a type of armor called chain mail, made of tiny metal rings linked together.

By the 15th and 16th centuries, knights wore improved armor made of heavy metal plates that covered them entirely. Even their heads were covered, by metal helmets with visors that could be pulled down to cover their face.

These suits of armor were so heavy that the knights had to be lifted onto their horses. If the knight fell off during battle, the weight of the armor made it impossible for him to get up, leaving him at his enemy's mercy.

With the arrival of guns in the 17th century, metal armor was given up in favor of lighter uniforms.

How did Indians hunt buffalo before they had horses?

Before they had horses, the Plains Indians hunted buffalo on foot.

One method involved dressing up in buffalo skins and creeping close enough to the herd to shoot the animals with arrows.

Another hunting method was to trap the herd inside a circle of fire with one exit. The hunters waited just outside the opening and killed the buffalo as they tried to escape.

The most effective way of surrounding a buffalo herd was to build a V-shaped runway out of stones and branches with the narrow end leading into a corral. The buffalo herd was coaxed into the wide end of the runway and then frightened by the Indians, causing it to stampede into the corral. Once inside, the buffalo were slaughtered.

If there was a cliff nearby the Indians sometimes built the same type of V-shaped runway leading to the cliff's edge. The buffalo would stampede down the runway and run over the edge of the cliff. Any buffalo not killed in the fall would be clubbed or shot with arrows.

DID YOU KNOW . . . the Indians used every part of the buffalo, including its tail as a fly swatter.

Why did Indians carve totem poles?

Your parents probably keep a photo album filled with photos that tell the story of your family —where you've gone and what you've done.

West Coast Indians had their own way of recording such events. They carved their stories on large tree trunks, which they placed in front of their house. These tall, wooden carvings are called totem poles.

Most totem poles show the symbol, or totem, of the family or tribe. The totem could be a bird, fish, animal or plant and would be carved on the very top of the pole.

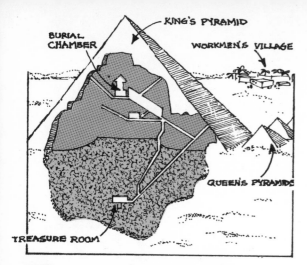

BURIAL CHAMBER

KING'S PYRAMID

WORKMEN'S VILLAGE

QUEEN'S PYRAMID

TREASURE ROOM

Why were the pyramids built?

The pyramids were built as tombs to house the bodies of ancient Egyptian kings, the pharaohs. The ancient Egyptians believed that a person's soul lived forever and that it needed its body in the life after death. They carefully preserved the bodies of their rulers, making them into mummies. Then they buried them in huge structures made of stone, with a square base and four triangular sides coming to a point at the top: the pyramids.

The most famous pyramids are those built along the Nile River in Egypt. The biggest is the Great Pyramid of Khufu at Giza. It covers an area of 5.3 hectares (13 acres) and is 147 metres (482 feet) high.

Where is the Valley of the Kings?

The pyramids were built so big and of such thick stone to protect the bodies of the pharaohs and to protect the treasure that was buried with them. But thieves usually managed to find a way in eventually, no matter how strongly built a pyramid was.

The solution, when found at last, was a simple one: hide the burial places of the kings.

The site chosen was a narrow gorge near the ancient city of Thebes, on the Nile. The place came to be called the Valley of the Kings, and there, hidden from searching eyes, the pharaohs' bodies and treasure lay undisturbed for centuries.

In modern times these too were

discovered by archaeologists. One of the most exciting finds was that of the tomb of young King Tutankhamen. When it was opened it revealed a great untouched treasure of gold, jewels and art work.

But even more valuable than the gold in Tut's tomb was the knowledge that the discovery gave us about how the ancient Egyptians lived and died.

What is a mummy?

A mummy is a well-preserved dead body. The ancient Egyptians in particular were very interested in preserving dead bodies because they believed that your body would still be needed in the life after death. The preserving process was not a quick one—it sometimes took up to 70 days to complete.

First they removed the organs, washed the body and stuffed it with spices. Then they applied a substance called natron (sodium carbonate) to help dry the body out.

When the body had dried it was wrapped in layers of cloth and placed in a casket, often shaped like the body it was to hold. Bodies treated this way, and buried in tombs in the dry atmosphere of the desert, could last for many thousands of years.

Why is Pompeii famous?

One of the favorite vacation spots
for the ancient Romans was Pompeii, a
thriving trade center with a good port on
the Bay of Naples. The townspeople produced wine, oil,
perfume and even a famous fish sauce for export. And
wealthy people, attracted by the sunny climate, built
houses near the shore to enjoy the sea air.

Unfortunately, Pompeii was also located near Mount
Vesuvius, an active volcano, and one terrible day in
A.D. 79, Vesuvius erupted. Large rocks were hurled
into the air and crashed down onto the surrounding
countryside. The air filled with poisonous gas, and
slowly the city of Pompeii disappeared under a pile of
hot ash and cinders.

Archaeologists have now uncovered much of
Pompeii. It is once again possible to walk its ancient
cobbled streets and visit its buildings. You can
even see some of the people who once lived there.
The ash that buried them hardened around
their bodies. Archaeologists have
carefully cut some of the resulting
molds open and have been able to cast
plaster replicas of the people.

What are the Dead Sea Scrolls?

The Dead Sea Scrolls are very old writings which were discovered in caves on the northwestern shores of the Dead Sea. They were written by a group of Jews who studied religion between the second century B.C. and the first century A.D. They contain parts of almost all the books of the Old Testament. The Dead Sea Scrolls are the oldest known copies of any of the books in the Bible.

The first group of scrolls was discovered in 1947 by a shepherd boy looking for a lost goat. He threw a stone into a cave and heard something shatter. When he looked to see what he had broken, he found the remains of a large clay jar containing several papyrus scrolls tied up with leather.

The remaining scrolls were found by archaeologists investigating the shepherd boy's find. This discovery contributed to our knowledge of Jewish and Christian history.

DID YOU KNOW . . . Vesuvius is an active volcano and has erupted more than 20 times since it destroyed Pompeii.

DID YOU KNOW . . .
Queen Elizabeth II is descended from the Vikings.

Who were the Vikings?

The Vikings were the early inhabitants of the area of Europe that is now Scandinavia. They were many things: explorers, settlers of new lands, pirates, great sailors and ship builders and fierce warriors.

During the Dark Ages the Vikings came from the North and explored and pillaged throughout southern Europe and across the Atlantic. The first European visitors to North America were Vikings. Their longships were among the most seaworthy boats ever designed, and in them they could go anywhere—and they did.

They set up colonies in parts of Europe, including the area of France known as Normandy. Later, as Normans, they went on to conquer England (in 1066) and to found kingdoms in Sicily and Calabria.

What was the Underground Railroad?

The Underground Railroad wasn't underground and it wasn't even a railroad. It was a network of escape routes used in the 1800s by black slaves traveling from the southern "slave" states in the United States to the northern free states and to Canada.

They used railroad terms for code words. Hiding places were "stations" and people who helped transport the escaping slaves were "conductors."

From 1830 to 1860, the Underground Railroad helped thousands to escape slavery and

How did America get its name?

Did you know that two great continents are named after one man? He was an Italian, Amerigo Vespucci.

Vespucci was an explorer and an expert navigator who, between 1497 and 1503, sailed on at least two expeditions along the coast of what is now called South America.

In 1507, a German mapmaker was drawing a map of the New World. He needed a name for the lands that had been discovered, and he had heard of the voyages of Americus Vespucius (the Latinized form of Vespucci's name). So he decided to name the lands after him and wrote "America" on the map. Other mapmakers followed his example —and the name stuck.

At first "America" was used only for South America, but later it came to be used for both continents: North and South America. Today, "America" is often used to mean just the United States of America.

Do you think that one explorer deserved to have two continents named after him? What would you have named the new continents?

start new lives as free citizens. Levi Coffin, the "president" of the railroad, helped more than 3000 slaves. His home was a station on three major escape routes. Harriet Tubman, a runaway slave herself, was the most famous black leader of the Underground Railroad. She risked her own freedom and returned to the south 19 times, helping about 300 blacks escape.

Who were the Aztecs?

The Aztecs were a powerful Indian tribe who lived in central Mexico. When the Spanish conqueror Hernán Cortés arrived in Tenochtitlan (now Mexico City) in 1519, he found a city with a population of more than 200 000—larger than any in Spain.

The Aztecs built elaborate houses, canals, roadways and magnificent temples that they decorated with carved gold sculptures. They were very advanced in other ways—they had an accurate calendar and a system of writing. The Aztecs kept slaves—often captured in war—but the children of slaves were born free. Their favorite sport was a game something like basketball, where players hit the ball into a hoop with their hips.

After the Spanish conquest in the 1500s, the Aztec Empire was destroyed and all the beautiful architecture and artworks were lost.

Who were the Mayas?

The decline of the Mayan civilization remains one of the great mysteries of all time. The land inhabited by the Mayas included large parts of present-day Mexico and Central America but their civilization was concentrated in the Yucatan Peninsula. This was one of the best agricultural areas in the region. The soil was so rich that it gave them corn in abundance and left them lots of time for other activities.

Famous for their architecture, the Mayas built magnificent stone pyramids and houses, and made beautiful stone carvings and pottery. They wove stunning garments of cotton and decorated their hair with the colorful feathers of tropical birds.

The Mayas had very advanced systems of mathematics and astrology and a calendar that was remarkably accurate. Like our own it was based on the orbit of the earth around the sun and a year was 365 days long.

The Mayan civilization flourished between A.D. 300 and 900. Shortly thereafter, these people mysteriously began to abandon their cities and return to live in the jungle. Perhaps someday the reason for this will be found. Maybe even by you!

What was the Black Death?

Can you die of a flea bite? You can if the flea is infected with the bubonic plague germ. Around 1347, a terrible epidemic plague —called the Black Death—spread through Europe. Whole villages, towns and cities were wiped out.

No one knew then that the Black Death was caused by fleas that had bitten infected rats, and later bit people. The signs of the disease were swelling, high fever, and bleeding under the skin that caused dark spots. Doctors were helpless.

The Black Death destroyed one quarter of the population of Europe and about one third of the inhabitants of England in less than 20 years.

What happened to the Titanic?

They said the *Titanic* was unsinkable. The luxurious British ocean liner was the largest ship of its kind and the fastest afloat.

On April 10, 1912, the *Titanic* set out on its first voyage, from England to New York, with 2223 passengers. Visibility was limited but it steamed along, trying to set a transatlantic record.

Shortly before midnight on April 14, the liner collided with an iceberg 153 kilometres (95 miles) south of Newfoundland. A great gash was ripped in its side, and ocean water rushed in. There was chaos and confusion as hysterical passengers rushed to board the few lifeboats. At 2:20 A.M., the *Titanic* sank with

832 passengers and 685 crew still aboard.

The liner *Californian* was quite near, but her radio operator was asleep. The *Carpathia,* 90 kilometres (56 miles) away, heard the *Titanic*'s distress signal, sped to the scene and picked up over 700 survivors. The sinking of the *Titanic,* one of the worst disasters in marine history, resulted in stricter laws for safety at sea.

How did the Great Fire of London start?

The Great Fire seems to have started in the shop of the king's baker in Pudding Lane near London Bridge. It was about three o'clock in the morning on September 1, 1666. At first it looked as though it would burn itself out, but a strong wind fanned the smoldering fire at the baker's, sending sparks to the thatched stables of a neighboring inn. By daylight, the Great Fire was underway as flames raged through the wooden houses and straw roofs.

The only fire-fighting equipment at that time consisted of little hand pumps, buckets and long hooks for pulling off thatch. Frightened Londoners loaded their possessions onto barges to escape the fire by river. A few stayed behind, pulling down houses to prevent the flames from spreading, but the fire moved too quickly. The wind blew burning scraps as far as 50 kilometres (30 miles) away!

After four terrifying days the fire died down. Most of London, the main port and largest city in the country, was in ashes and smoking ruins. To prevent such a disaster from ever happening again, the city was rebuilt using brick and stone.

Who was Cleopatra?

You have probably heard of Cleopatra. She was one of the most famous queens that ever lived. But it might surprise you to learn that there were actually *seven* queens of Egypt called Cleopatra. Only one, however—the last one—became really famous.

The famous Cleopatra lived from 69 to 30 B.C. She was the last of the line of Ptolemies who had ruled Egypt for almost 300 years. She was intelligent, witty and ambitious and she had charms that brought two of the world's most powerful men into her arms.

Cleopatra became queen of Egypt in 51 B.C. when her father, Ptolemy XII Auletes, died. Under the terms of his will, she was to share the rule with her ten-year-old brother. The following year her brother's guardians seized the throne in an attempt to make him sole ruler of Egypt. A bitter civil war followed, and as it raged Julius Caesar, ruler of Rome, came to Egypt. Caesar fell in love with Cleopatra and used his armies to defeat her brother. Cleopatra was again put on the throne of Egypt, this time ruling with another younger brother.

In 46 B.C. Cleopatra went to Rome with Caesar. When he was assassinated two years later, she returned and arranged the murder of her brother.

Shortly thereafter she met

Mark Antony, who had been Caesar's friend and who was now one of the three men who together ruled the Roman Empire. Antony fell madly in love with Cleopatra and married her in 37 B.C. She hoped to rule Rome as Antony's queen.

Antony began to spend more and more time away from Rome in Egypt with Cleopatra. He gave Roman land to her sons and grew less interested in Roman politics. This angered the Roman senate and citizens, who felt he was neglecting his duties. War broke out, and Antony and Cleopatra were defeated in a sea battle off the coast of Greece in 31 B.C.

Following the defeat, Cleopatra locked herself in the mausoleum she had ordered built for her own funeral. She tricked Antony into committing suicide by sending him a message that she had killed herself.

The clever Cleopatra then tried to captivate Octavian, who had become sole ruler of Rome. But this time her charms didn't work. Octavian planned to take her to Rome, but not as his queen. He was going to exhibit her in a wooden cage as a traitor. The proud Cleopatra preferred to die.

Legend claims that Cleopatra had an asp (a poisonous snake that was the symbol of ancient Egypt) smuggled to her in a basket of figs. She placed the asp on her arm and died of its poisonous bite.

What is the Rosetta Stone?

Can you learn a language from a stone? One man did—from the Rosetta Stone.

The stone was found by a French officer in Napoleon's army in 1799, half-buried in the mud near Rosetta, Egypt. It was a slab of black rock 28 centimetres (11 inches) thick, 114 centimetres (45 inches) tall and 72 centimetres (28 inches) wide. And it was covered with carved inscriptions: 14 lines of Egyptian hieroglyphics (picture writing); 32 lines of Egyptian demotic (a simpler version of the hieroglyphics); and 54 lines of Greek.

The language of ancient Egypt had long been a riddle to scholars, but the Rosetta Stone provided the key to solving it. A French scholar, Jean Champollion, translated the Greek, and guessed that the hieroglyphic and demotic writing said the same as the Greek. Using the Greek and Egyptian words he recognized as a guide, Champollion figured out

how to read the hieroglyphics and published the results in 1822. This enabled scholars to translate other ancient Egyptian writings for the first time.

What did the Rosetta Stone say? It was carved by Egyptian priests to commemorate the crowning of Ptolemy V, king of Egypt from 203–181 B.C.

DID YOU KNOW . . . 230 000 troops fought in the Battle of Waterloo and there were 49 000 casualties.

Who fought the Battle of Waterloo?

When someone meets with a great defeat or failure have you ever heard people say that he has "met his Waterloo?" This comes from the fact that the Battle of Waterloo was the end of everything for the Emperor Napoleon.

Napoleon, the emperor of France, had dominated Europe for almost ten years when he was thrown out by an alliance of the other nations of Europe. He managed to escape from exile and regain power in 1815, but his triumph lasted only 100 days. Challenged once again by the European allies, Napoleon gathered an army and marched it north to do battle against a British-German-Dutch force led by the Duke of Wellington.

The armies met on a sunny day in June at the village of Waterloo in Belgium. They fought all day without either side gaining the advantage. Then the Prussian troops arrived and attacked the French from behind.

Napoleon was destroyed. He gave himself up to the British who sent him live in exile on the tiny island of St. Helena in the south Atlantic. He stayed there until his death.

Napoleon truly met his Waterloo that day: a defeat from which he never recovered!

What was the Ice Age?

The last great Ice Age ended about 10 000 years ago. During that time, the whole of Canada, except for a few corners, was covered by a sheet of ice that was as much as 3 kilometres (2 miles) thick. Vast glaciers also covered part of the United States, and much of Europe and Russia.

When the Ice Age began, the earth got colder and the great glaciers in the north began to grow southward. The expanding ice sheets moved slowly, destroying forests, tearing away the surface of the earth and spreading the Arctic cold as far south as Illinois in North America. Nobody knows why the glaciers spread over the earth. We do believe that there have been four ice ages in the last quarter of a million years, and that there were probably other ice ages even longer ago.

We have an idea of how many ice ages there have been because each time the glaciers come down from the north they leave a trail of changes in the shape of the land. For example, the Great Lakes were dug out by a glacier. And since scientists are able to tell how old the various land forms are, they can tell when there were ice ages that caused changes.

DID YOU KNOW . . . frozen mammoths have been found in the ice of Siberia, perfectly preserved, with frozen flowers still between their teeth.

What was a mammoth?

There are only two kinds of elephant now, the African and the Asian, but there used to be other kinds. Mammoths were elephants that lived in the north. Elephants today have very little hair, but the mammoths had short, thick fur covering their bodies, and an outer layer of long, black, woolly hair.

Mammoths lived during the last Ice Age, so they needed all that fur. They lived in dense northern forests, and on the tundras that lay along the edges of huge glaciers. Mammoths looked a lot like elephants, except for their woolly coats and small ears. One kind of mammoth, the Imperial Mammoth, was bigger than the modern elephant. Our Stone-Age ancestors hunted mammoths; the last ones in Canada died about 10 000 years ago.

What was the Renaissance?

The word "renaissance" means rebirth. The Renaissance was a time in European history when there were a lot of changes in the way people thought. At this time, during the 15th and 16th centuries, writings of the ancient Greeks and Romans were rediscovered, and their ideas were given a new life.

In the previous centuries, called the Middle Ages, the Christian Church was the major influence on how people thought. During the Renaissance, people began to question the Church.

Out of all this questioning came a lot of creativity. This was a time of great writing and painting. The Renaissance began in Italy and the most famous artists of the period are Italian: Botticelli, Leonardo da Vinci, Michelangelo...

The best-known English figure of the time was William Shakespeare, whose plays are still interesting and fresh to us today.

What were the Wars of the Roses?

Roses don't fight—men do. In the late 1400s, two great rival families fought for the English throne. They were the House of York (the white rose) and the House of Lancaster (the red rose). The different roses helped to identify each side and gave the struggle its name: the "Wars of the Roses."

The wars began in 1455 with the Battle of St. Albans, which the Yorkists won, and ended in

What were the Middle Ages?

The Middle Ages were the centuries between the fall of the Roman Empire and the Renaissance. This time is often called the "Age of Faith," because the Church had such a strong influence on daily life in Europe.

There were three classes of people: the nobles who governed, the clergy who dealt with religious matters, and the common people who worked to support the first two classes. The gap between rich and poor was enormous.

Although there were some wars, crusades and peasant revolts, life in the Middle Ages was pretty quiet. Towns grew and prospered. New industries started up, and trade and exploration brought luxury goods to Europe from all corners of the world. Skilled craftsmen built magnificent castles and cathedrals, thousands of which are still standing today.

1485 with the Battle of Bosworth, which gave final victory to the Lancastrians. During this time there were violent battles and many secret murders. Many nobles were killed.

After the victory at Bosworth, Henry Tudor, the leader of the House of Lancaster, became King Henry VII. Realizing that the two great families had almost destroyed each other with this senseless rivalry, he wisely married Elizabeth of the House of York, to unite the warring houses.

What was the longest war ever fought?

The longest war ever was probably the Hundred Years War, which actually lasted even longer than a hundred years.

The war broke out in 1337, when Edward III, the king of England, invaded France. Edward owned almost half of France, so he thought he should rule it instead of the French king, Philip VI.

England invaded France many times, its armies marching back and forth over the country. The war continued long after Edward and Philip died. Crops and houses were destroyed in many parts of France, leaving the people with nothing to eat and nowhere to live.

But no matter how many times the French were defeated in battle, they never gave up. Finally, in 1453, the war was won by the French King Charles VII, the great-great-grandson of Philip VI.

DID YOU KNOW . . . the Chinese began carrying cloth flags similar to the ones we have today as early as 1100 B.C.

What country has the oldest flag?

The oldest flag of any modern country belongs to Denmark. Denmark has flown the same flag for over 750 years. According to legend, in about 1219 the Danish King Waldemar saw a white cross blazing in a blood-red sky as he led his troops into battle against the pagans. Waldemar took this as a sign that God wanted Denmark to win the battle. Denmark was victorious, and ever since then the Danish flag has been a white cross on a red background.

How did pirates live?

The word "pirate" means sea robber. Since ancient times pirates have sailed the seas and oceans looking for ships to rob. The great age of piracy lasted from the 1500s through the 1700s. During this time, peaceful sailing ships were often at the mercy of ruthless pirates who killed or captured crews and stole precious cargoes.

Pirates often hid on tiny islands or along coastlines. Islands in the Caribbean Sea and off the Spanish Main (the mainland of South America) were popular pirate hideouts. The pirates of the Spanish Main were called buccaneers because they cured their meat on *boucans,* or wooden grills.

Most of the men who became pirates were cruel and lawless. But even the most ruthless pirates obeyed certain laws of the sea. Pirate crews shared their booty equally. And they were usually loyal to each other, and would take good care of sick or wounded shipmates.

29

Why was the Great Wall of China built?

Imagine a wall 2400 kilometres (1500 miles) long, snaking like a dragon's back over mountains and into ravines of very rugged country. This is the Great Wall of China, the longest wall in the world.

In the early days, Mongolian hordes from the north were constantly attacking China. Stretches of wall were built, but the Mongolians still poured in. In 221 B.C., the Emperor Chin Shih Huang Ti sent his best general north with 300 000 soldiers to drive out the invaders and to build a continuous wall across the northern provinces—from Tibet to the Yellow Sea.

They began by joining the earlier walls, doing all the work by hand. The workers were forced laborers: prisoners of war, peasants and criminals. Thousands of them died while building the Wall. Their bones were crushed and buried under it. Some people called it "the longest cemetery in the world."

The Great Wall was built wide enough so that six horses could gallop together along the top, and it is 5 to 10 metres (16 to 32 feet) high.

Over the centuries, the Great Wall has been extended, knocked down and built up again. Some sections no longer exist, but it remains one of the wonders of the world.

DID YOU KNOW . . . the Great Wall was the only manmade construction American astronauts could identify from space.